This book is presented to:

_____

From:_____

Date:_____

ISBN

9781736764350

JoAnn Dotson Blue Light Publishing

www.authorjoanndotson.com

BedTime

Thank you Lord for parents and grandparents too!

Keep me safe and warm as I sleep in you. Amen

Laying down to sleep in my bed

Is my daily bread

As my head lay on this pillow

I bless your Holy Name.

Amen

Sleep, sleep come to me
Thank you Jesus,
It's you that's in me.

Amen

It's my mama and daddy and me
God, I thank you for all three
Now as I lay down to sleep
I am grateful for our peace.

Amen

I love my mama and daddy too

Thank you Lord for all you do!

Dinner Time

We are grateful for this food,

And it's all because of you!

Amen

Hallelujah!

For our food

This is the highest praise we can give to you.

A light unto my feet

A lamp unto my path

I thank you Lord

For our daily bread.

Obeying My Parents

Obeying my parents
In all that I do
I know oh God,
This pleases you!

Gratefulness

Lord, I'm grateful for my toys

Please help my parents keep a job!

School Prayer

As I enter and exit this
school year.
This one thing I know.
You are my protection,
50 feet above
And 50 feet below
50 feet on all sides,
You are my covering Host!

Be Tall in me Jesus

While I am at school

On the playgrounds, classrooms, and halls

Protect me Father,

FROM ANY DOWNFALLS!

Amen

Goodnight Jesus!

www.ingramcontent.com/pod-product-compliance
Lightning Source LLC
Chambersburg PA
CBHW042112040426

42448CB00002B/240